Merry Christmas
Julian
Love ya!
Uncle Jerry & Aunt Arlene 12/2017

Fun Stuff

Cupcakes

Publications International, Ltd.

Louis Weber, CEO
Publications International, Ltd.
7373 North Cicero Avenue
Lincolnwood, IL 60712

Recipe development on pages 22, 28, 34, 44, 46, 62, 72, 78, 84, 86, 88, 104, 116, 118 and 122 by Lauren Smekhov.

Front cover photography and photography on pages 7, 13, 15, 23, 27, 29, 35, 37, 43, 45, 47, 63, 65, 73, 79, 85, 87, 89, 95, 101, 105, 115, 117, 119, 123 and 109 by PIL Photo Studio.
Photographer: Annemarie Zelasko
Photographer's Assistant: Lauren Kessler
Food Stylists: Kathryn Joy, Carol Smoler
Assistant Food Stylists: Elaine Funk, Sheila Grannen

Pictured on the front cover *(clockwise from top left):* Friendly Ghost Cupcakes *(page 54),* Easter Chicks *(page 48),* Mini Bees *(page 16)* and Sweet Little Sheep *(page 4).*
Pictured on the jacket flaps: Sailboat Cupcakes *(page 28)* and Sweetheart Strawberry Cupcakes *(page 44).*
Pictured on the back cover *(left to right):* Orange Dreamsicle Cupcakes *(page 24),* Crazy Colors Cupcakes *(page 26)* and Bittersweet Chocolate Raspberry Cupcakes *(page 104).*

ISBN-13: 978-1-4508-4927-2
ISBN-10: 1-4508-4927-X

Library of Congress Control Number: 2012930252

Manufactured in China.

8 7 6 5 4 3 2 1

Microwave Cooking: Microwave ovens vary in wattage. Use the cooking times as guidelines and check for doneness before adding more time.

Publications International, Ltd.

Contents

Cupcake Cuties

Sweet Little Sheep

1 package (about 18 ounces) cake mix, any flavor, plus ingredients to prepare mix
1 container (16 ounces) white frosting
2 packages (10½ ounces each) mini marshmallows

Chewy chocolate candies
Small round white and pink decors
Black decorating gel

1. Preheat oven to 350°F. Line 60 mini (1¾-inch) muffin cups with paper baking cups. Prepare cake mix according to package directions. Spoon batter into prepared muffin cups, filling almost full.

2. Bake 10 minutes or until toothpick inserted into centers comes out clean. Cool cupcakes in pans 10 minutes; remove to wire racks to cool completely.

3. Frost cupcakes. Press marshmallows into frosting, completely covering cupcakes.

4. Unwrap chewy chocolate candies; cut off and reserve small piece of each candy to use for ears. Working with one large piece at a time, microwave on LOW (30%) 5 seconds or until slightly softened. For heads, press candy between hands or on waxed paper to flatten slightly; form into oblong shape. For ears, cut reserved small pieces of candy in half. Shape each half into triangle.

5. Press candy head into one side of each cupcake. Press candy ears onto top of head. Attach decors for eyes and noses using small amount of frosting. Pipe dot of decorating gel in each eye.

Makes 60 mini cupcakes

Koala Cupcakes

1 package (about 18 ounces) cake mix, any flavor, plus ingredients to prepare mix
1 container (16 ounces) white frosting
   Black food coloring
   White chocolate candy discs
   Jumbo pink confetti sprinkles
   Small round white candies
   Black jelly beans or chocolate-covered raisins
   Black decorating gel

1. Preheat oven to 350°F. Line 22 standard (2½-inch) muffin cups with paper baking cups. Prepare cake mix according to package directions. Spoon batter into prepared muffin cups, filling two-thirds full.

2. Bake 20 minutes or until toothpick inserted into centers comes out clean. Cool cupcakes in pans 10 minutes; remove to wire racks to cool completely.

3. Place frosting in medium microwavable bowl. Add food coloring, a few drops at a time, until desired shade of gray is reached. Microwave on HIGH about 10 seconds or until very soft but not completely melted. Dip tops of cupcakes in frosting to coat; let stand on wire racks until set.

4. Press candy discs into sides of cupcakes for ears; frost tops of discs. Place sprinkle in center of each disc. Attach white candies for eyes and jelly beans for noses. Pipe dot of decorating gel in each eye. Place remaining frosting in piping bag fitted with star tip; pipe frosting on tops of cupcakes to resemble fur. *Makes 22 cupcakes*

Koala Cupcakes

Leopard Spots

1 package (about 18 ounces) dark chocolate cake mix, plus ingredients to prepare mix
3 cups powdered sugar, sifted
½ cup (1 stick) butter, softened
3 to 4 tablespoons milk, divided
½ teaspoon vanilla
Brown and yellow food coloring
Black and orange decorating gels

1. Preheat oven to 350°F. Line 22 standard (2½-inch) muffin cups with paper baking cups. Prepare cake mix according to package directions. Spoon batter into prepared muffin cups, filling two-thirds full.

2. Bake 20 minutes or until toothpick inserted into centers comes out clean. Cool cupcakes in pans 10 minutes; remove to wire racks to cool completely.

3. Beat powdered sugar, butter, 2 tablespoons milk and vanilla in large bowl with electric mixer at low speed until blended. Beat at high speed until light and fluffy, adding additional milk, 1 teaspoon at a time, to reach spreading consistency. Add food coloring, a few drops at a time, to create sandy color. Frost cupcakes.

4. Pipe spots all over tops of cupcakes with black decorating gel for outline and orange decorating gel in centers.

Makes 22 cupcakes

Leopard Spots

Pink Piglets

1 package (about 18 ounces) yellow cake mix, plus ingredients to prepare mix
1 container (16 ounces) white frosting
   Pink or red food coloring
   Mini semisweet chocolate chips
   Small fruit-flavored pastel candy wafers
   Red or pink chewy fruit candy squares

1. Preheat oven to 350°F. Line 60 mini (1¾-inch) muffin cups with paper baking cups. Prepare cake mix according to package directions. Spoon batter into prepared muffin cups, filling almost full.

2. Bake 10 minutes or until toothpick inserted into centers comes out clean. Cool cupcakes in pans 10 minutes; remove to wire racks to cool completely.

3. Place frosting in medium bowl; add food coloring, a few drops at a time, until desired shade of pink is reached. Frost cupcakes. Create faces at one side of each cupcake using chocolate chips for eyes and candy wafers for noses.

4. Working with one at a time, unwrap candy squares and microwave on LOW (30%) 5 to 10 seconds or until softened. Press candy between hands or on waxed paper to flatten to ⅛-inch thickness. Use scissors or paring knife to cut out triangles for ears; fold over top corner of each triangle. Arrange ears on cupcakes.

5. Cut ⅛-inch strips, 1 to 2 inches long, from flattened candies. Shape candy strips into spirals for tails; place candies in freezer 10 minutes to set. Place tails on cupcakes.

Makes 60 mini cupcakes

Pink Piglets

Ladybug Cupcakes

1 package (about 18 ounces) cake mix, any flavor, plus ingredients to prepare mix
1 container (16 ounces) white frosting
  Red food coloring
  Chocolate-covered mint candies, chocolate malt balls or other round chocolate candies
  Black string licorice
  Mini semisweet chocolate chips
  White and black decorating icings

1. Preheat oven to 350°F. Line 22 standard (2½-inch) muffin cups with paper baking cups. Prepare cake mix according to package directions. Spoon batter into prepared muffin cups, filling two-thirds full.

2. Bake 20 minutes or until toothpick inserted into centers comes out clean. Cool cupcakes in pans 10 minutes; remove to wire racks to cool completely.

3. Place frosting in medium microwavable bowl. Add food coloring, a few drops at a time, until desired shade of red is reached. Microwave on HIGH about 10 seconds or until very soft but not completely melted. Dip tops of cupcakes in frosting to coat; let stand on wire racks until set.

4. Press chocolate candy into one end of each cupcake for head. Cut licorice into 2½-inch lengths; press into center of each cupcake running from head to opposite side. Arrange chocolate chips, point ends down, all over each cupcake. Pipe eyes and mouths with decorating icings.

Makes 22 cupcakes

Tip To get the ladybug spots to lay flat, cut the pointed tips off the chocolate chips with a small paring knife.

Ladybug Cupcakes

Kittycakes

1 package (about 18 ounces) cake mix, any flavor, plus ingredients to prepare mix
  White and pink candy wafers
  Black string licorice
1 container (16 ounces) white frosting
  Black food coloring
  Chocolate-covered sunflower seeds or mini candy-coated chocolate pieces
  Pink heart decors
  Black decorating icing

1. Preheat oven to 350°F. Line 22 standard (2½-inch) muffin cups with paper baking cups. Prepare cake mix according to package directions. Spoon batter into prepared muffin cups, filling two-thirds full.

2. Bake 20 minutes or until toothpick inserted into centers comes out clean. Cool cupcakes in pans 10 minutes; remove to wire racks to cool completely.

3. Use paring knife to cut candy wafers into triangles for ears. Cut licorice into 1-inch lengths for whiskers. (Cut licorice strings in half lengthwise if thinner whiskers are desired.)

4. Reserve ½ cup frosting in small bowl. Place remaining frosting in medium microwavable bowl. Microwave on HIGH about 10 seconds or until very soft but not completely melted. Dip tops of cupcakes in frosting to coat; let stand on wire racks until set.

5. Add food coloring, a few drops at a time, to reserved frosting until desired shade of gray is reached. Place frosting in piping bag fitted with small round tip; pipe frosting on tops and sides of cupcakes. Place wafer ears and licorice whiskers on cupcakes. Attach sunflower seeds for eyes and heart decors for noses. Pipe mouths and pupils with decorating icing.

Makes 22 cupcakes

Kittycakes

Mini Bees

    1 package (about 18 ounces) chocolate cake mix, plus ingredients to prepare mix
    1 container (16 ounces) chocolate frosting
    1½ cups prepared white frosting
       Yellow food coloring
       Black string licorice
       Yellow candy wafers

1. Preheat oven to 350°F. Line 60 mini (1¾-inch) muffin cups with paper baking cups. Prepare cake mix according to package directions. Spoon batter into prepared muffin cups, filling almost full.

2. Bake 10 minutes or until toothpick inserted into centers comes out clean. Cool cupcakes in pans 10 minutes; remove to wire racks to cool completely.

3. Place chocolate frosting in medium microwavable bowl. Microwave on HIGH about 10 seconds or until very soft but not completely melted. Dip tops of cupcakes in frosting to coat; let stand on wire racks until set. Reserve remaining chocolate frosting.

4. Place white frosting in medium bowl; add food coloring, a few drops at a time, until desired shade of yellow is reached. Place frosting in piping bag fitted with small round tip or resealable food storage bag with ⅛-inch corner cut off. Pipe stripes on cupcakes.

5. Place reserved chocolate frosting in separate piping bag or resealable food storage bag; pipe eyes and mouths on cupcakes. Cut licorice into 1½-inch lengths; place on cupcakes just above eyes for antennae and at opposite side for stingers. Cut candy wafers in half; arrange two halves on each cupcake for wings. *Makes 60 mini cupcakes*

Mini Bees

Zebra Stripes

1 package (about 18 ounces) dark chocolate cake mix, plus ingredients to prepare mix
24 ounces white chocolate
8 ounces whipping cream
Black decorating icing

1. Preheat oven to 350°F. Line 22 standard (2½-inch) muffin cups with paper baking cups. Prepare cake mix according to package directions. Spoon batter into prepared muffin cups, filling two-thirds full.

2. Bake 20 minutes or until toothpick inserted into centers comes out clean. Cool cupcakes in pans 10 minutes; remove to wire racks to cool completely.

3. Chop white chocolate; place in medium heatproof bowl. Heat cream to a simmer in small saucepan over medium heat; pour over chocolate. Let stand 5 minutes; stir until blended and smooth. Let stand 5 minutes or until slightly thickened.

4. Dip tops of cupcakes in glaze to coat; let stand on wire racks until set.

5. Pipe stripes on tops of cupcakes with decorating icing.

Makes 22 cupcakes

Zebra Stripes

Party Pleasers

Strawberry Milkshake Cupcakes

2 cups all-purpose flour

1½ cups granulated sugar

4 teaspoons baking powder

½ teaspoon salt

1¼ cups (2½ sticks) butter, softened, divided

1 cup plus 6 to 8 tablespoons milk, divided

2 teaspoons vanilla, divided

3 eggs

2 containers (7 ounces each) plain Greek yogurt

1 cup seedless strawberry preserves

6 cups powdered sugar, divided

¼ cup shortening

Pink food coloring

Assorted pastel sugar pearls and decorating sugar

1. Preheat oven to 350°F. Line 24 standard (2½-inch) muffin cups with paper baking cups.

2. Beat flour, granulated sugar, baking powder and salt in large bowl with electric mixer at low speed until blended. Add ½ cup butter; beat at medium speed 30 seconds. Add 1 cup milk and 1 teaspoon vanilla; beat 2 minutes. Add eggs; beat 2 minutes. Spoon batter evenly into prepared muffin cups.

3. Bake 20 minutes or until toothpick inserted into centers comes out clean. Cool cupcakes in pans 10 minutes; remove to wire racks to cool completely.

4. For filling, combine yogurt and preserves in medium bowl. Transfer to piping bag fitted with medium round tip. Press tip into top of each cupcake and squeeze bag to fill.

5. Beat 3 cups powdered sugar, remaining ¾ cup butter, shortening, 4 tablespoons milk and remaining 1 teaspoon vanilla in large bowl with electric mixer at low speed until smooth. Add remaining 3 cups powdered sugar; beat until light and fluffy, adding remaining milk, 1 tablespoon at a time, as needed for desired consistency. Add food coloring, a few drops at a time, until desired shade of pink is reached. Pipe or spread frosting on cupcakes. Decorate as desired.

Makes 24 cupcakes

Honey Roasted Peanut Butter Minis

1¼ cups all-purpose flour
1 teaspoon baking powder
¼ teaspoon salt
⅔ cup packed brown sugar
½ cup creamy peanut butter
¼ cup vegetable oil
1 egg
2 tablespoons honey
½ cup milk
⅔ cup chopped honey roasted peanuts, divided
Honey Peanut Butter Frosting (recipe follows)

1. Preheat oven to 350°F. Line 28 mini (1¾-inch) muffin cups with paper baking cups.

2. Combine flour, baking powder and salt in small bowl. Combine brown sugar, peanut butter, oil, egg and honey in large bowl; stir until well blended and smooth. Add flour mixture and milk; mix just until combined. Stir in ⅓ cup chopped peanuts. Spoon batter evenly into prepared muffin cups.

3. Bake 15 minutes or until toothpick inserted into centers comes out clean. Cool cupcakes in pans 5 minutes; remove to wire racks to cool completely.

4. Prepare Honey Peanut Butter Frosting. Pipe or spread frosting on cupcakes; sprinkle with remaining ⅓ cup chopped peanuts.   *Makes 28 mini cupcakes*

Honey Peanut Butter Frosting: Combine ⅔ cup creamy peanut butter, ¼ cup (½ stick) softened butter and ¼ cup honey in large bowl; stir until smooth. Stir in 1 cup powdered sugar until well blended.

Honey Roasted Peanut Butter Minis

Orange Dreamsicle Cupcakes

1½ cups all-purpose flour
1½ (0.15-ounce) envelopes orange unsweetened drink mix
2 teaspoons baking powder
⅛ teaspoon salt
1 cup granulated sugar
1 cup (2 sticks) butter, softened, divided
2 eggs
½ cup plus 3 tablespoons milk, divided
1½ teaspoons vanilla, divided
3 cups powdered sugar
Orange food coloring
White sprinkles

1. Preheat oven to 350°F. Line 12 standard (2½-inch) muffin cups with paper baking cups.

2. Whisk flour, drink mix, baking powder and salt in small bowl. Beat granulated sugar and ½ cup butter in medium bowl with electric mixer at medium speed until creamy. Add eggs, one at a time, beating well after each addition. Add flour mixture; beat until blended. Add ½ cup milk and 1 teaspoon vanilla; beat until smooth. Spoon batter evenly into prepared muffin cups.

3. Bake 20 minutes or until toothpick inserted into centers comes out clean. Cool cupcakes in pan 10 minutes; remove to wire rack to cool completely.

4. Beat powdered sugar, remaining ½ cup butter, 3 tablespoons milk and ½ teaspoon vanilla in large bowl with electric mixer at medium speed until fluffy. Add food coloring, a few drops at a time, until desired shade of orange is reached. Frost cupcakes; decorate with sprinkles.

Makes 12 cupcakes

Orange Dreamsicle Cupcakes

Crazy Colors Cupcakes

1 package (about 18 ounces) white cake mix
1 cup sour cream
3 eggs
½ cup vegetable oil
Gel food coloring (4 colors)
1 container (16 ounces) white or cream cheese frosting
Mini rainbow candy-coated chocolate chips

1. Preheat oven to 325°F. Line 20 standard (2½-inch) muffin cups with white paper baking cups.

2. Beat cake mix, sour cream, eggs and oil in large bowl with electric mixer at low speed 30 seconds. Beat at medium speed 2 minutes or until well blended. Divide batter evenly among four medium bowls; tint each bowl with different color food coloring. (Batter colors should be strong to retain color after baking.)

3. Spoon layer of one color batter into each prepared cup (about 2 teaspoons); spread batter to edge of cup with back of spoon or dampened fingers. Top with second color batter, making sure to completely cover first layer. Repeat with remaining two colors of batter. (If desired, switch order of colored layers halfway though assembly.)

4. Bake 18 to 20 minutes or until toothpick inserted into centers comes out clean. Cool cupcakes in pans 10 minutes; remove to wire racks to cool completely.

5. Frost cupcakes; decorate with rainbow chocolate chips.   *Makes 20 cupcakes*

Tips: Use as few or as many colors as you like for the rainbow layers and adjust the amount of batter in each cup accordingly. For faster layering of the different color batters, place each color batter into a disposable piping bag or plastic food storage bag with one corner cut off and pipe the layers into muffin cups instead of using a spoon.

Crazy Colors Cupcakes

Sailboat Cupcakes

11 chocolate peanut butter cups
16 squares white chocolate (2 [4-ounce] bars), divided
   Red, white and blue sprinkles or decors
 1 package (about 18 ounces) cake mix, any flavor, plus ingredients to prepare mix
 3 cups powdered sugar
⅓ cup boiling water
½ teaspoon vanilla
¼ teaspoon salt
 1 cup (2 sticks) butter, cut into pieces, softened
¼ cup shortening
   Blue food coloring

1. Cut peanut butter cups in half. Cut 11 white chocolate squares in half diagonally with sharp knife to create 22 triangles.

2. Place remaining 5 squares white chocolate in small microwavable bowl. Microwave on HIGH at 30-second intervals, stirring after each interval, until melted and smooth. Attach white chocolate sails to peanut butter cup boats using small amount of melted white chocolate. Lay sailboats on parchment paper 1 hour or until set. Decorate with sprinkles, using melted white chocolate to attach.

3. Preheat oven to 350°F. Line 22 standard (2½-inch) muffin cups with paper baking cups. Prepare and bake cupcakes according to package directions. Cool cupcakes in pans 5 minutes; remove to wire racks to cool completely.

4. Beat powdered sugar, boiling water, vanilla and salt in large bowl with electric mixer at low speed until smooth and cool. Add butter and shortening; beat at medium-high speed 3 minutes or until doubled in volume. Add food coloring, a few drops at a time, until desired shade of blue is reached.

5. Pipe frosting waves on cupcakes using piping bag fitted with star tip. Top cupcakes with sailboats.

Makes 22 cupcakes

Sailboat Cupcakes

Billiard Ball Cupcakes

 1 package (about 18 ounces) cake mix, any flavor, plus ingredients to prepare mix
6 cups powdered sugar, divided
 1 cup (2 sticks) butter, softened
6 to 8 tablespoons milk, divided
 1 teaspoon vanilla
   Assorted food coloring
   White wafer candy discs
   Black decorating gel

1. Preheat oven to 350°F. Line 22 standard (2½-inch) muffin cups with paper baking cups. Prepare cake mix according to package directions. Spoon batter into prepared muffin cups, filling two-thirds full.

2. Bake 20 minutes or until toothpick inserted into centers comes out clean. Cool cupcakes in pans 10 minutes; remove to wire racks to cool completely.

3. Beat 3 cups powdered sugar, butter, 4 tablespoons milk and vanilla in large bowl with electric mixer at low speed until smooth. Add remaining 3 cups powdered sugar; beat until light and fluffy, adding remaining milk, 1 tablespoon at a time, as needed for spreadable consistency.

4. Reserve one fourth of frosting. Divide remaining frosting evenly among small bowls; add different food coloring to each bowl, a few drops at a time, until desired shades are reached.

5. For "solids," frost cupcakes with colored frosting. Place one candy disc in center of each cupcake. For "stripes," frost cupcakes with reserved white frosting. Spread center two thirds of each cupcake with colored frosting. Place one candy disc in center of each cupcake.

6. Pipe number in center of each candy disc with decorating gel.   *Makes 22 cupcakes*

Billiard Ball Cupcakes

Whoopie Pie Cupcakes

  1 package (about 18 ounces) dark chocolate cake mix, plus ingredients to prepare mix
½ cup (1 stick) butter, softened
¼ cup shortening
  3 cups powdered sugar
⅓ cup whipping cream
  1 teaspoon salt

1. Preheat oven to 350°F. Grease 22 standard (2½-inch) muffin cups. Prepare cake mix according to package directions. Spoon batter into prepared muffin cups, filling two-thirds full.

2. Bake 20 minutes or until toothpick inserted into centers comes out clean. Cool cupcakes in pans 10 minutes; remove to wire racks to cool completely.

3. Beat butter and shortening in large bowl with electric mixer at medium speed until well blended. Add powdered sugar, cream and salt; beat at low speed 1 minute. Beat at medium-high speed 2 minutes or until fluffy.

4. Slice tops off cupcakes. Spread filling over bottoms of cupcakes; replace tops.

Makes 22 cupcakes

Whoopie Pie Cupcakes

Furry Monsters

Cupcakes

- 1½ cups all-purpose flour
- 1 teaspoon baking powder
- ½ teaspoon baking soda
- ½ teaspoon salt
- ½ cup (1 stick) butter, softened
- 1 cup granulated sugar
- 2 eggs
- Grated peel and juice of 1 lemon
- ½ cup buttermilk

Frosting

- 2½ cups powdered sugar
- Juice of 2 lemons
- 2 tablespoons boiling water
- ¼ teaspoon salt
- ¾ cup (1½ sticks) butter, cut into pieces, softened
- Blue and green food coloring
- Assorted candies and black string licorice
- Black decorating gel

1. Preheat oven to 350°F. Line 12 standard (2½-inch) muffin cups with paper baking cups.

2. For cupcakes, combine flour, baking powder, baking soda and ½ teaspoon salt in medium bowl. Beat ½ cup butter and granulated sugar in large bowl with electric mixer at medium speed until creamy. Add eggs, peel and juice of 1 lemon; beat until well blended. Add flour mixture; beat at low speed while adding buttermilk. Beat just until combined. Spoon batter into prepared muffin cups, filling two-thirds full.

3. Bake 20 to 22 minutes or until toothpick inserted into centers comes out clean. Cool cupcakes in pan 5 minutes; remove to wire rack to cool completely.

4. For frosting, beat powdered sugar, juice of 2 lemons, boiling water and ¼ teaspoon salt in large bowl with electric mixer at low speed until smooth and cool. Add ¾ cup butter; beat at medium-high speed 3 minutes or until doubled in volume. Divide frosting between two bowls; add food coloring, a few drops at a time, until desired shades are reached.

5. Pipe fur on cupcakes using piping bag fitted with star tip. Decorate cupcakes with candies and licorice to create monster faces. Pipe dot of decorating gel in each eye.

Makes 12 cupcakes

Triple Scoop Cupcakes

  1 cup all-purpose flour
¾ cup sugar
  2 teaspoons baking powder
¼ teaspoon salt
¼ cup (½ stick) butter, softened
⅓ cup milk
½ teaspoon vanilla
  2 eggs
½ (16-ounce) container white or cream cheese frosting
    Butter waffle cookies
    Pastel-colored thin candy wafers
    Jumbo confetti sprinkles

1. Preheat oven to 350°F. Line 12 standard (2½-inch) muffin cups with paper baking cups.

2. Beat flour, sugar, baking powder and salt in large bowl with electric mixer at low speed until blended. Add butter; beat at medium speed 30 seconds. Add milk and vanilla; beat 2 minutes. Add eggs; beat 2 minutes. Spoon batter evenly into prepared muffin cups.

3. Bake 20 minutes or until toothpick inserted into centers comes out clean. Cool cupcakes in pan 10 minutes; remove to wire rack to cool completely.

4. Frost cupcakes. Use paring knife to cut 1½-inch-long triangles from butter cookies to resemble ice cream cones. Place one triangle on each cupcake; top with three candy wafers. Decorate edges of cupcakes with sprinkles. *Makes 12 cupcakes*

Triple Scoop Cupcakes

Cupcake Teepees

1 package (9 ounces) cake mix, any flavor, plus ingredients to prepare mix
1 jar (7½ ounces) marshmallow creme
24 fruit rollups

1. Preheat oven to 350°F. Spray 40 mini (1¾-inch) muffin cups with nonstick cooking spray. Prepare cake mix according to package directions. Spoon batter into prepared muffin cups, filling half full.

2. Bake 12 minutes or until toothpick inserted into centers comes out clean. Cool cupcakes in pans 5 minutes; remove to wire racks to cool completely.

3. Turn cupcakes upside down on large serving platter. Spoon 1 tablespoon marshmallow creme on top of each cupcake.

4. Unwrap and unroll fruit rollups; lay flat on work surface. Cut 20 circles from fruit rollups using 4-inch stiff paper or cardboard circle as template. Cut each circle in half.

5. To form teepee, place center of round side of one half-circle at bottom of one cupcake; wrap ends around cupcake. Repeat with remaining fruit rollups and cupcakes. Serve immediately.

Makes 40 mini cupcakes

Variation: Experiment with different flavors of cake, fruit rollups and fillings. For a strawberry shortcake flavor, use white cake mix, whipped cream instead of marshmallow creme and strawberry-flavored fruit rollups.

Cupcake Teepees

Blue Suede Cupcakes

2¼ cups all-purpose flour
1 teaspoon salt
2 bottles (1 ounce each) blue food coloring
3 tablespoons unsweetened cocoa powder
1 cup buttermilk
1 teaspoon vanilla
1½ cups granulated sugar
1 cup (2 sticks) butter, softened, divided
2 eggs
1 teaspoon white vinegar
1 teaspoon baking soda
1 package (8 ounces) cream cheese, softened
3 cups powdered sugar
2 tablespoons milk
Additional blue food coloring
Blue decorating sugar

1. Preheat oven to 350°F. Line 20 standard (2½-inch) muffin cups with paper baking cups.

2. Whisk flour and salt in medium bowl. Gradually stir food coloring into cocoa in small bowl until blended and smooth. Combine buttermilk and vanilla in another small bowl.

3. Beat granulated sugar and ½ cup butter in large bowl with electric mixer at medium speed 4 minutes or until light and fluffy. Add eggs, one at a time, beating well after each addition. Add cocoa mixture; beat until well blended. Add flour mixture alternately with buttermilk mixture, beating just until blended. Stir vinegar into baking soda in small bowl; gently fold into batter (do not use mixer). Spoon batter evenly into prepared muffin cups.

4. Bake 20 minutes or until toothpick inserted into centers comes out clean. Cool cupcakes in pans 10 minutes; remove to wire racks to cool completely.

5. Beat remaining ½ cup butter and cream cheese in large bowl with electric mixer at medium-high speed until smooth. Gradually beat in powdered sugar at low speed. Beat in milk until blended. Add additional food coloring, a few drops at a time, until desired shade of blue is reached. Frost cupcakes; sprinkle with decorating sugar. *Makes 20 cupcakes*

Blue Suede Cupcakes

Letter Cupcakes

      3 cups all-purpose flour
      2 teaspoons baking powder
    ½ teaspoon salt
  1½ cups sugar
    ½ cup (1 stick) butter, softened
      2 eggs
      1 teaspoon vanilla
      1 cup sour cream
      1 container (16 ounces) white frosting
      Jumbo rainbow nonpareils

1. Preheat oven to 350°F. Line 24 standard (2½-inch) muffin cups with paper baking cups.

2. Whisk flour, baking powder and salt in medium bowl. Beat sugar and butter in large bowl with electric mixer at medium speed 2 to 3 minutes or until light and fluffy. Add eggs, one at a time, beating well after each addition. Stir in vanilla. Add flour mixture alternately with sour cream, beating just until blended. Spoon batter evenly into prepared muffin cups.

3. Bake 20 to 25 minutes or until toothpick inserted into centers comes out clean. Cool cupcakes in pans 10 minutes; remove to wire racks to cool completely.

4. Place frosting in medium microwavable bowl; microwave on HIGH about 10 seconds or until very soft but not completely melted. Dip tops of cupcakes in frosting to coat; let stand on wire racks until set.

5. Use tweezers to place nonpareils on cupcakes to create letters and words.

Makes 24 cupcakes

Letter Cupcakes

Seasonal Sweets

Sweetheart Strawberry Cupcakes

1 cup coarsely chopped strawberries, divided
1½ cups all-purpose flour
1 teaspoon baking powder
½ teaspoon baking soda
½ teaspoon salt
¾ cup granulated sugar

½ cup (1 stick) butter, softened
2 eggs
1 teaspoon vanilla
⅓ cup buttermilk
Tangy Strawberry Buttercream (recipe follows)
6 small strawberries, halved

1. Preheat oven to 350°F. Line 12 standard (2½-inch) muffin cups with paper baking cups. Place ¾ cup chopped strawberries in food processor; process until smooth. Reserve 2 tablespoons strawberry purée for frosting.

2. Combine flour, baking powder, baking soda and salt in medium bowl. Beat granulated sugar and butter in large bowl with electric mixer at medium speed until creamy. Add ½ cup strawberry purée until blended. Add eggs and vanilla; beat well. Add flour mixture; beat at low speed while adding buttermilk. Beat just until combined. Stir in remaining ¼ cup chopped strawberries. Spoon batter into prepared muffin cups, filling two-thirds full.

3. Bake 20 to 22 minutes or until toothpick inserted into centers comes out clean. Cool cupcakes in pan 5 minutes; remove to wire rack to cool completely.

4. Prepare Tangy Strawberry Buttercream. Pipe or spread frosting on cupcakes. Cut strawberry halves to resemble hearts; top cupcakes with strawberry hearts.   *Makes 12 cupcakes*

Tangy Strawberry Buttercream: Beat ½ cup (1 stick) softened butter, 4 ounces softened cream cheese and 2 tablespoons reserved strawberry purée in large bowl with electric mixer at medium speed until well blended. Gradually add 2 to 2½ cups powdered sugar; beat until desired consistency is reached.

Kiss Me Cupcakes

    1 cup white chocolate candy discs
      Hot pink decorating sugar
1¼ cups all-purpose flour
1½ teaspoons baking powder
  1 teaspoon baking soda
½ teaspoon salt
  1 cup granulated sugar
½ cup plus ¾ teaspoon vegetable oil, divided
  2 eggs
½ cup milk
1½ cups (9 ounces) semisweet chocolate chips
    Chocolate sprinkles

1. Draw at least 12 (2-inch) sets of lips on sheet of parchment paper with marker. Turn paper over; place on baking sheet. (You should be able to see outlines of lips through paper.) Melt candy discs according to package directions. Place melted white chocolate in plastic squeeze bottle or piping bag fitted with small round tip. Pipe lips on parchment paper using outlines as guide; immediately sprinkle with decorating sugar. Let stand until set.

2. Preheat oven to 350°F. Line 12 standard (2½-inch) muffin cups with paper baking cups.

3. Combine flour, baking powder, baking soda and salt in small bowl. Combine granulated sugar, ½ cup oil and eggs in large bowl; whisk until well blended. Add flour mixture and milk; stir until blended. Spoon batter evenly into prepared muffin cups.

4. Bake 25 minutes or until toothpick inserted into centers comes out clean. Cool cupcakes in pan 5 minutes; remove to wire rack to cool completely.

5. Combine chocolate chips and remaining ¾ teaspoon oil in medium microwavable bowl. Microwave on HIGH at 30-second intervals, stirring after each interval, until melted and smooth.

6. Place chocolate sprinkles in shallow bowl. Dip tops of cupcakes in melted chocolate, then in sprinkles. Top cupcakes with lips. Let stand on wire rack until set. *Makes 12 cupcakes*

Kiss Me Cupcakes

Easter Chicks

1 package (about 18 ounces) yellow cake mix, plus ingredients to prepare mix
2 containers (16 ounces each) white frosting
Pink and yellow food coloring
Orange chewy fruit candy squares
Black decorating gel

1. Preheat oven to 350°F. Line 60 mini (1¾-inch) muffin cups with paper baking cups. Prepare cake mix according to package directions. Spoon batter into prepared muffin cups, filling almost full.

2. Bake 10 minutes or until toothpick inserted into centers comes out clean. Cool cupcakes in pans 5 minutes; remove to wire racks to cool completely. Use serrated knife to cut off rounded domes of cupcakes so tops are flat.

3. Divide frosting between two small bowls; add food coloring, a few drops at a time, until desired shades are reached.

4. Remove baking cups from half of cupcakes. Spread small amount of frosting (about ½ teaspoon) in center of cupcakes with baking cups. Set remaining cupcakes (without baking cups) upside down over frosting; press gently to seal cupcakes together. Frost cupcakes in desired colors, mounding extra frosting on top to create egg shape.

5. Working with one at a time, unwrap candy squares and microwave on LOW (30%) 5 to 10 seconds or until softened. Press candy between hands or on waxed paper to flatten to ⅛-inch thickness. Use scissors or paring knife to cut out triangles for beaks. Create faces on chicks with candy beaks and dots of decorating gel for eyes.   *Makes 30 mini cupcakes*

Easter Chicks

Mini Fireworks

1 package (about 18 ounces) chocolate cake mix, plus ingredients to prepare mix
4 ounces almond bark or white chocolate candy discs
   Red, white and blue decorating sugar
1 container (16 ounces) chocolate frosting

1. Preheat oven to 350°F. Line 60 mini (1¾-inch) muffin cups with paper baking cups. Prepare cake mix according to package directions. Spoon batter into prepared muffin cups, filling almost full.

2. Bake 10 minutes or until toothpick inserted into centers comes out clean. Cool cupcakes in pans 5 minutes; remove to wire racks to cool completely.

3. Place large piece of waxed paper on work surface. Melt almond bark according to package directions; place in plastic squeeze bottle or piping bag fitted with small round tip. Pipe firework shapes on waxed paper, a few at a time; immediately sprinkle with decorating sugar. Repeat to create 60 large or 120 small fireworks. Let stand until set.

4. Frost cupcakes; top with fireworks.

Makes 60 mini cupcakes

Mini Fireworks

All-American Cupcakes

1 package (about 18 ounces) cake mix, any flavor, plus ingredients to prepare mix
1 container (16 ounces) white frosting
  Blue candy stars
  Red string licorice

1. Preheat oven to 350°F. Line 22 standard (2½-inch) muffin cups with paper baking cups. Prepare cake mix according to package directions. Spoon batter into prepared muffin cups, filling two-thirds full.

2. Bake 20 minutes or until toothpick inserted into centers comes out clean. Cool cupcakes in pans 10 minutes; remove to wire racks to cool completely.

3. Frost cupcakes. Arrange candy stars in left corner of each cupcake. Arrange licorice in rows across remaining portion of each cupcake, cutting pieces to fit. *Makes 22 cupcakes*

Tip Blue candy stars can be found in the bulk section of candy stores and at some craft stores. If you can't find them, you can substitute mini candy-coated chocolate pieces or blue candy dots.

All-American Cupcakes

Friendly Ghost Cupcakes

1⅓ cups all-purpose flour
¾ cup unsweetened cocoa powder
2 teaspoons baking powder
½ teaspoon salt
¼ teaspoon baking soda
1 cup sugar
6 tablespoons (¾ stick) butter, softened
2 eggs
1 teaspoon vanilla
¾ cup milk
1 cup prepared chocolate frosting
4 cups whipped topping
Mini semisweet chocolate chips

1. Preheat oven to 350°F. Line 14 standard (2½-inch) muffin cups with paper baking cups.

2. Whisk flour, cocoa, baking powder, salt and baking soda in medium bowl. Beat sugar and butter in large bowl with electric mixer at medium speed until fluffy. Add eggs and vanilla; beat until well blended. Add flour mixture and milk; beat at low speed just until combined. Spoon batter evenly into prepared muffin cups.

3. Bake 15 minutes or until toothpick inserted into centers comes out clean. Cool cupcakes in pans 10 minutes; remove to wire racks to cool completely.

4. Place frosting in medium microwavable bowl. Microwave on HIGH about 10 seconds or until very soft but not completely melted. Dip tops of cupcakes in frosting to coat; let stand on wire racks until set.

5. Place whipped topping in piping bag fitted with large round tip or resealable food storage bag with 1 inch cut off one corner of bag. Pipe ghost shape onto each cupcake (or drop whipped topping by spoonfuls onto cupcakes to resemble ghosts); add chocolate chips for eyes. Refrigerate until ready to serve.

Makes 14 cupcakes

Friendly Ghost Cupcakes

Mummy Cakes

  1 package (about 18 ounces) chocolate cake mix, plus ingredients to prepare mix
¼ cup plus 3 tablespoons unsweetened cocoa powder, divided
  1 teaspoon ground cinnamon
  1 teaspoon ground ginger
  1 package (about 16 ounces) refrigerated sugar cookie dough, softened
  4 cups powdered sugar
⅓ cup plus 1 tablespoon milk
  2 tablespoons butter, softened
     Small red cinnamon candies
½ cup chocolate cookie crumbs

1. Preheat oven to 350°F. Line 22 standard (2½-inch) muffin cups with paper baking cups. Prepare cake mix according to package directions. Spoon batter into prepared muffin cups, filling two-thirds full.

2. Bake 20 minutes or until toothpick inserted into centers comes out clean. Cool cupcakes in pans 10 minutes; remove to wire racks to cool completely.

3. Knead ¼ cup cocoa, cinnamon and ginger into cookie dough on lightly floured work surface until well blended. Roll out dough to ¼-inch thickness. Cut out shapes using 3-inch gingerbread man cookie cutter; place on ungreased cookie sheets. Bake 7 minutes or until edges are set. Remove cookies to wire racks to cool completely.

4. Beat powdered sugar, milk and butter in large bowl with electric mixer at medium speed until creamy. Place about one third of frosting in medium resealable food storage bag with small tip cut from one corner. Attach two cinnamon candies to face of each cookie for eyes using small amount of frosting. Pipe frosting across cookies for mummy wrappings. Let stand until frosting is set.

5. Add remaining 3 tablespoons cocoa to remaining frosting; stir until blended. Frost cupcakes; sprinkle with cookie crumbs. Top cupcakes with cookies.   *Makes 22 cupcakes*

Mummy Cakes

Dracula Cupcakes

1 package (about 18 ounces) white cake mix, plus ingredients to prepare mix
1 container (16 ounces) white frosting
   Black decorating gel
   Yellow decorating gel
   Red decorating gel
   White decorating icing

1. Preheat oven to 350°F. Line 22 standard (2½-inch) muffin cups with paper baking cups.

2. Prepare and bake cupcakes according to package directions. Cool cupcakes in pans 10 minutes; remove to wire racks to cool completely.

3. Frost cupcakes with white frosting.

4. Pipe hair and outline of eyes and noses with black decorating gel. Pipe eyes with yellow decorating gel; pipe dot of black gel in each eye.

5. Pipe mouths with red decorating gel. Pipe fangs with white decorating icing.

Makes 22 cupcakes

Dracula Cupcakes

Sweet Potato Spice Cupcakes

1¼ pounds sweet potatoes, quartered
1½ cups all-purpose flour
1¼ cups granulated sugar
2 teaspoons baking powder
1 teaspoon ground cinnamon
½ teaspoon baking soda
½ teaspoon salt
¼ teaspoon ground allspice
¾ cup vegetable oil
2 eggs
½ cup chopped walnuts or pecans, plus additional for garnish
½ cup raisins
Cream Cheese Frosting (recipe follows)

1. Place sweet potatoes in large saucepan; cover with water. Cover and cook over medium heat 30 minutes or until fork-tender. Drain sweet potatoes; peel and mash when cool enough to handle.

2. Preheat oven to 325°F. Line 18 standard (2½-inch) muffin cups with paper baking cups.

3. Whisk flour, granulated sugar, baking powder, cinnamon, baking soda, salt and allspice in medium bowl. Beat mashed sweet potatoes (about 2 cups), oil and eggs in large bowl with electric mixer at low speed until blended. Add flour mixture; beat at medium speed 30 seconds or until well blended. Stir in ½ cup walnuts and raisins. Spoon batter evenly into prepared muffin cups.

4. Bake 20 minutes or until toothpick inserted into centers comes out clean. Cool cupcakes in pans 10 minutes; remove to wire racks to cool completely.

5. Prepare Cream Cheese Frosting. Frost cupcakes; sprinkle with additional walnuts. Store covered in refrigerator. *Makes 18 cupcakes*

Cream Cheese Frosting: Beat 1 package (8 ounces) softened cream cheese, ¼ cup (½ stick) softened butter, ¼ teaspoon salt and ¼ teaspoon vanilla in medium bowl with electric mixer at medium-high speed until creamy. Gradually beat in 1½ cups sifted powdered sugar until well blended.

Sweet Potato Spice Cupcakes

Pumpkin Pie Surprise Cupcakes

1 package (18 ounces) yellow cake mix, plus ingredients to prepare mix
1 teaspoon ground cinnamon
1 refrigerated (9-inch) pie crust
3 cups whipping cream
1½ cups canned pumpkin pie filling
Ground nutmeg (optional)

1. Preheat oven to 350°F. Line 22 standard (2½-inch) muffin cups with paper baking cups.

2. Prepare and bake cupcakes according to package directions, stirring cinnamon into batter. Cool cupcakes in pans 10 minutes; remove to wire racks to cool completely.

3. Meanwhile, prepare pumpkin cutouts. *Increase oven temperature to 400°F.* Line baking sheet with parchment paper. Unroll pie crust on work surface; use cookie cutter or paring knife to cut out 22 small (1- to 2-inch) pumpkins. Place cutouts on prepared baking sheet; score 4 vertical lines in each pumpkin to resemble ridges in pumpkins. Bake 10 minutes or until light golden brown. Remove cutouts to wire rack to cool completely.

4. Beat cream in large bowl with electric mixer at medium-high speed until stiff peaks form. Combine 1 cup whipped cream and pumpkin pie filling in medium bowl; mix well.

5. Cut hole in top of each cupcake (about 1 inch wide and 1 inch deep); discard cupcake pieces. Fill each hole with about 1 tablespoon pumpkin filling. Pipe or spread remaining whipped cream over filling; sprinkle lightly with nutmeg, if desired. Top cupcakes with pumpkin cutouts.

Makes 22 cupcakes

Pumpkin Pie Surprise Cupcakes

Double Gingerbread Cupcakes

1¾ cups all-purpose flour
1 teaspoon ground cinnamon
1 teaspoon ground ginger
¾ teaspoon salt, divided
½ teaspoon baking soda
½ teaspoon ground allspice
¾ cup (1½ sticks) butter, softened, divided
½ cup packed brown sugar
3 tablespoons molasses
1 egg
1 package (14½ ounces) gingerbread cake and cookie mix,* plus ingredients to prepare mix
White decorating icing
Red decors (optional)
1 package (8 ounces) cream cheese, softened
2 cups sifted powdered sugar

*If gingerbread cake mix is not available, substitute spice cake mix; add 2 teaspoons ground ginger to batter. Spice cake mix will make 22 to 24 cupcakes; use 12 for this recipe and reserve remaining cupcakes for another use.

1. Combine flour, cinnamon, ginger, ½ teaspoon salt, baking soda and allspice in medium bowl. Beat ½ cup butter and brown sugar in large bowl with electric mixer at medium speed about 5 minutes or until light and fluffy. Beat in molasses and egg until well blended. Beat in flour mixture at low speed until well blended. Divide dough in half; wrap and refrigerate at least 2 hours or up to 24 hours.**

2. Meanwhile, prepare cupcakes. Preheat oven to 350°F. Line 12 standard (2½-inch) muffin cups with paper baking cups. Prepare cake mix according to package directions for cake; spoon batter evenly into prepared muffin cups. Bake about 20 minutes or until toothpick inserted into centers comes out clean. Cool cupcakes in pan 10 minutes; remove to wire rack to cool completely.

3. Line cookie sheets with parchment paper. Roll out half of dough to ⅛-inch thickness on lightly floured surface. Cut out shapes using 1½-inch gingerbread man cookie cutter. Place cutouts 1 inch apart on prepared cookie sheets.

4. Bake about 5 minutes or until edges are lightly browned. Cool cookies on cookie sheets 1 minute; remove to wire racks to cool completely. Decorate cooled cookies using decorating icing and decors, if desired.

5. Beat cream cheese, remaining ¼ cup butter and ¼ teaspoon salt in medium bowl with electric mixer at medium-high speed until creamy. Gradually beat in powdered sugar until well blended. Frost cupcakes; top with cookies. *Makes 12 cupcakes*

**Only half of dough is needed for cupcake toppers. Remaining dough may be refrigerated or frozen for later use.

Sweet Snowflakes

1 package (about 18 ounces) white cake mix, plus ingredients to prepare mix
4 ounces almond bark or white chocolate candy discs
White or blue sugar pearls, white nonpareils and coarse sugar
1 container (16 ounces) white frosting

1. Preheat oven to 350°F. Line 22 standard (2½-inch) muffin cups with paper baking cups. Prepare cake mix according to package directions. Spoon batter into prepared muffin cups, filling two-thirds full.

2. Bake 20 minutes or until toothpick inserted into centers comes out clean. Cool cupcakes in pans 10 minutes; remove to wire racks to cool completely.

3. Place large piece of waxed paper on work surface. Melt almond bark according to package directions; place in plastic squeeze bottle or piping bag fitted with small round tip. Pipe snowflake shapes on waxed paper, a few at a time; immediately decorate with sugar pearls, nonpareils and coarse sugar as desired. Repeat to create 22 large or 44 small snowflakes. Let stand until set.

4. Pipe or spread frosting on cupcakes. Roll edges of frosting in nonpareils, if desired. Top cupcakes with snowflakes.

Makes 22 cupcakes

Sweet Snowflakes

Snowy Peaks

1 package (about 18 ounces) chocolate cake mix, plus ingredients to prepare mix
4 egg whites, at room temperature
6 tablespoons sugar

1. Preheat oven to 350°F. Line 9 jumbo (3½-inch) muffin cups with paper baking cups. Prepare cake mix according to package directions. Spoon batter into prepared muffin cups, filling two-thirds full.

2. Bake 20 to 25 minutes or until toothpick inserted into centers comes out clean. Cool cupcakes in pans 10 minutes; remove to wire racks to cool completely.

3. *Increase oven temperature to 375°F.* Beat egg whites in medium bowl with electric mixer at high speed until soft peaks form. Gradually add sugar, beating until stiff peaks form. Pipe or spread meringue on each cupcake.

4. Place cupcakes on baking sheet. Bake 5 minutes or until peaks of meringue are golden.

Makes 9 jumbo cupcakes

Tip Egg whites reach the fullest volume if they are allowed to stand at room temperature for 30 minutes before beating. Make sure that the bowl and beaters you are using are clean and dry, as any traces of grease or yolk will decrease the volume of the egg whites. For best results, use a copper, stainless steel or glass bowl (plastic bowls have an oily film even after repeated washings).

Snowy Peaks

Fresh Flavors

Cannoli Cupcakes

2 cups all-purpose flour
½ teaspoon baking powder
½ teaspoon baking soda
½ teaspoon salt
1 cup granulated sugar
½ cup (1 stick) butter, softened
1 cup whole-milk ricotta cheese
1 teaspoon grated orange peel

1 egg
2 teaspoons vanilla, divided
1 cup whipping cream
8 ounces mascarpone cheese, softened
½ cup powdered sugar
Mini semisweet chocolate chips and chopped unsalted pistachios

1. Preheat oven to 350°F. Line 15 standard (2½-inch) muffin cups with paper baking cups.

2. Whisk flour, baking powder, baking soda and salt in small bowl. Beat granulated sugar and butter in large bowl with electric mixer at medium speed until creamy. Add ricotta cheese and orange peel; beat until blended. Add egg and 1 teaspoon vanilla; beat until well blended. Add flour mixture; beat until blended. Spoon batter evenly into prepared muffin cups.

3. Bake 20 minutes or until toothpick inserted into centers comes out clean. Cool cupcakes in pans 10 minutes; remove to wire racks to cool completely.

4. Beat cream in medium bowl with electric mixer at high speed until stiff peaks form. Combine mascarpone cheese, powdered sugar and remaining 1 teaspoon vanilla in another medium bowl. Fold whipped cream into mascarpone mixture until blended.

5. Frost cupcakes; sprinkle with chocolate chips and pistachios.   *Makes 15 cupcakes*

Mojito Minis

Cupcakes

- ¾ cup all-purpose flour
- ½ teaspoon baking powder
- ½ teaspoon baking soda
- ¼ teaspoon salt
- ½ cup granulated sugar
- ¼ cup (½ stick) butter, softened
- 1 egg
- Grated peel and juice of 1 lime
- ¼ cup milk
- 2 to 4 tablespoons white rum, divided
- ¼ cup chopped fresh mint

Frosting

- 2½ cups powdered sugar
- Juice of 2 limes
- ¾ cup (1½ sticks) butter, cut into cubes, softened
- 2 tablespoons chopped fresh mint

1. Preheat oven to 350°F. Line 18 mini (1¾-inch) muffin cups with paper baking cups.

2. For cupcakes, combine flour, baking powder, baking soda and salt in small bowl. Beat granulated sugar and ¼ cup butter in large bowl with electric mixer at medium speed until fluffy. Add egg, peel and juice of 1 lime; beat until well blended. Add flour mixture, milk and 2 tablespoons rum; beat just until combined. Stir in ¼ cup mint. Spoon batter into prepared muffin cups, filling three-fourths full.

3. Bake 15 minutes or until toothpick inserted into centers comes out clean. Brush warm cupcakes with remaining 2 tablespoons rum, if desired. Remove to wire racks to cool completely.

4. For frosting, beat powdered sugar and juice of 2 limes in large bowl with electric mixer at medium speed until well blended. Add ¾ cup butter; beat at high speed 3 minutes or until thick and fluffy. Stir in 2 tablespoons mint. Pipe or spread frosting on cupcakes.

Makes 18 mini cupcakes

Mojito Minis

Maple Bacon Cupcakes

Cupcakes

- 1½ cups all-purpose flour
- 1¾ teaspoons baking powder
- ¾ cup granulated sugar
- ½ cup (1 stick) butter, softened
- 2 eggs
- 2 tablespoons maple syrup
- ½ cup milk
- 8 slices bacon, crisp-cooked and finely chopped, divided

Maple Frosting

- ½ cup (1 stick) butter, softened
- 3 tablespoons maple syrup
- 2 tablespoons milk
- 3 cups powdered sugar

1. Preheat oven to 350°F. Line 12 standard (2½-inch) muffin cups with paper baking cups.

2. For cupcakes, whisk flour and baking powder in small bowl. Beat granulated sugar and ½ cup butter in large bowl with electric mixer at medium speed until light and fluffy. Add eggs and 2 tablespoons maple syrup; beat well. Add flour mixture and ½ cup milk; beat at low speed just until combined. Reserve 2 tablespoons bacon for topping. Stir remaining bacon into batter. Spoon batter evenly into prepared muffin cups.

3. Bake 20 minutes or until toothpick inserted into centers comes out clean. Cool cupcakes in pan 10 minutes; remove to wire rack to cool completely.

4. For frosting, beat ½ cup butter, 3 tablespoons maple syrup and 2 tablespoons milk in large bowl with electric mixer at low speed 1 minute. Add powdered sugar; beat at medium speed until fluffy. Frost cupcakes; top with reserved bacon. *Makes 12 cupcakes*

Maple Bacon Cupcakes

Chai Latte Cupcakes

    7 chai tea bags, divided
 1½ cups boiling water
    1 package (about 18 ounces) white cake mix
    3 eggs
 ⅓ cup vegetable oil
    1 cup milk
    2 to 3 cups powdered sugar
       Turbinado sugar (optional)

1. Place 4 tea bags in small bowl. Pour water over tea bags; let steep until slightly cooled. Squeeze tea bags; discard.

2. Preheat oven to 350°F. Line 22 standard (2½-inch) muffin cups with paper baking cups.

3. Beat cake mix, tea, eggs and oil in large bowl with electric mixer at medium speed 2 minutes or until well blended. Spoon batter evenly into prepared muffin cups.

4. Bake 20 minutes or until toothpick inserted into centers comes out clean. Cool cupcakes in pans 10 minutes; remove to wire racks to cool completely.

5. Bring milk to a simmer in small saucepan over medium heat; remove from heat. Add remaining 3 tea bags to milk; let steep until slightly cooled. Squeeze tea bags; discard. Whisk in powdered sugar until smooth and thick enough for dipping.

6. Dip tops of cupcakes in glaze; return to wire racks. Sprinkle with turbinado sugar, if desired. Let stand until set.

Makes 22 cupcakes

Chai Latte Cupcakes

Zucchini Basil Cupcakes

1¼ cups all-purpose flour
1½ teaspoons baking powder
1 teaspoon baking soda
½ teaspoon salt
1 cup granulated sugar
½ cup vegetable oil
2 eggs
½ cup milk
1 cup grated zucchini, pressed or squeezed to remove liquid
¼ cup finely chopped fresh basil
1 package (8 ounces) cream cheese, softened
¼ cup (½ stick) butter, softened
1¾ cups powdered sugar
1 teaspoon vanilla
Small whole fresh basil leaves (optional)

1. Preheat oven to 350°F. Line 16 standard (2½-inch) muffin cups with paper baking cups.

2. Combine flour, baking powder, baking soda and salt in small bowl. Whisk sugar, oil and eggs in large bowl until well blended. Add flour mixture and milk; mix well. Stir in zucchini and chopped basil. Spoon batter evenly into prepared muffin cups.

3. Bake 25 minutes or until toothpick inserted into centers comes out clean. Cool cupcakes in pans 5 minutes; remove to wire racks to cool completely.

4. Beat cream cheese and butter in large bowl with electric mixer at medium speed until well combined. Add powdered sugar and vanilla; beat at low speed 1 minute. Beat at medium-high speed 5 minutes or until fluffy.

5. Frost cupcakes; garnish with basil leaves.

Makes 16 cupcakes

Zucchini Basil Cupcakes

Chocolate Bourbon Bites

Cupcakes

1 package (about 18 ounces) devil's food cake mix without pudding in the mix
1 cup buttermilk*
3 eggs
⅓ cup bourbon
¼ cup (½ stick) butter, melted and cooled
1 cup mini semisweet chocolate chips

Frosting

3 cups powdered sugar
1 cup unsweetened cocoa powder
½ cup (1 stick) butter, softened
⅓ cup milk
¼ cup bourbon
1 teaspoon vanilla

If you don't have buttermilk, substitute 1 tablespoon vinegar or lemon juice plus enough milk to equal 1 cup. Let stand 5 minutes.

1. Preheat oven to 350°F. Line 60 mini (1¾-inch) muffin cups with paper baking cups.

2. For cupcakes, beat cake mix, buttermilk, eggs, ⅓ cup bourbon and ¼ cup butter in large bowl with electric mixer at low speed 30 seconds. Beat at medium speed 2 minutes or until well blended. Stir in chocolate chips. Spoon batter into prepared muffin cups, filling almost full.

3. Bake 10 minutes or until toothpick inserted into centers comes out clean. Cool cupcakes in pans 5 minutes; remove to wire racks to cool completely.

4. For frosting, beat powdered sugar, cocoa, ½ cup butter, milk, ¼ cup bourbon and vanilla in large bowl with electric mixer at medium speed until smooth. Frost cupcakes.

Makes 60 mini cupcakes

Chocolate Bourbon Bites

Blueberry Cupcakes with Goat Cheese Frosting

Cupcakes
- 1½ cups all-purpose flour
- 1¾ teaspoons baking powder
- ½ teaspoon salt
- ¾ cup granulated sugar
- ½ cup (1 stick) butter, softened
- 2 eggs
- 2 teaspoons vanilla
- ½ cup milk
- 1 cup fresh blueberries, plus additional for garnish

Goat Cheese Frosting
- 4 ounces goat cheese
- ¼ cup (½ stick) butter, softened
- 2 cups powdered sugar
- 2 tablespoons milk

1. Preheat oven to 350°F. Line 12 standard (2½-inch) muffin cups with paper baking cups.

2. For cupcakes, whisk flour, baking powder and salt in small bowl. Beat granulated sugar and ½ cup butter in large bowl with electric mixer at medium speed until light and fluffy. Add eggs and vanilla; beat well. Add flour mixture and ½ cup milk; beat at low speed just until combined. Stir in 1 cup blueberries. Spoon batter evenly into prepared muffin cups.

3. Bake 20 minutes or until toothpick inserted into centers comes out clean. Cool cupcakes in pan 10 minutes; remove to wire rack to cool completely.

4. For frosting, beat goat cheese and ¼ cup butter in large bowl with electric mixer at medium speed until well blended. Add powdered sugar and 2 tablespoons milk; beat until smooth. Frost cupcakes; garnish with additional blueberries. *Makes 12 cupcakes*

Blueberry Cupcakes with Goat Cheese Frosting

Salted Caramel Cupcakes

    1½ cups all-purpose flour
      1 teaspoon baking powder
    ½ teaspoon salt
      1 cup packed brown sugar
    ½ cup (1 stick) butter, softened
      2 eggs
      1 teaspoon vanilla
    ½ cup buttermilk
        Salted Caramel Frosting (recipe follows)
        Sea salt

1. Preheat oven to 325°F. Line 12 standard (2½-inch) muffin cups with paper baking cups.

2. Combine flour, baking powder and ½ teaspoon salt in small bowl. Beat brown sugar and ½ cup butter in large bowl with electric mixer at medium speed until fluffy. Add eggs and vanilla; beat until well blended. Add flour mixture and buttermilk; beat just until combined. Spoon batter evenly into prepared muffin cups.

3. Bake 20 to 25 minutes or until toothpick inserted into centers comes out clean. Cool cupcakes in pan 10 minutes; remove to wire rack to cool completely.

4. Prepare Salted Caramel Frosting. Pipe or spread frosting on cupcakes; sprinkle lightly with sea salt.

Makes 12 cupcakes

Salted Caramel Frosting

    ½ cup granulated sugar
      2 tablespoons water
    ¼ cup whipping cream
      1 teaspoon sea salt
      1 cup (2 sticks) butter, softened
    2½ cups powdered sugar

1. Heat granulated sugar and water in heavy saucepan over high heat, without stirring, until medium to dark amber in color. Remove from heat. Carefully stir in cream and 1 teaspoon sea salt (mixture will foam). Set aside to cool 15 minutes.

2. Beat 1 cup butter and caramel mixture in large bowl with electric mixer at medium-high speed until well blended. Add powdered sugar; beat until thick and creamy. (If frosting is too soft, refrigerate 10 minutes before piping or spreading on cupcakes.)

Spicy Coconut Lime Cupcakes

1¾ cups all-purpose flour
1½ teaspoons baking powder
1 teaspoon salt
½ teaspoon baking soda
½ teaspoon ground red pepper
¾ cup sugar
½ cup (1 stick) butter, softened
¾ cup canned coconut milk, well shaken
2 eggs
¼ cup milk
Grated peel and juice of 2 limes
⅓ cup sweetened flaked coconut
Coconut Lime Whipped Cream (recipe follows)
⅓ cup sweetened flaked coconut, toasted*
Additional grated lime peel (optional)

*To toast coconut, spread evenly in shallow baking pan. Bake in 350°F oven 5 to 7 minutes or until golden brown, stirring occasionally.

1. Preheat oven to 350°F. Line 12 standard (2½-inch) muffin cups with paper baking cups.

2. Combine flour, baking powder, salt, baking soda and ground red pepper in medium bowl. Beat sugar and butter in large bowl with electric mixer at medium speed until creamy. Add coconut milk, eggs, milk, lime peel and lime juice; beat until blended. Add flour mixture and ⅓ cup coconut; beat at low speed just until blended. Spoon batter evenly into prepared muffin cups.

3. Bake 18 to 20 minutes or until toothpick inserted into centers comes out clean. Cool cupcakes in pan 5 minutes; remove to wire rack to cool completely.

4. Prepare Coconut Lime Whipped Cream. Frost cupcakes; top with toasted coconut and additional lime peel, if desired. Store in refrigerator.   *Makes 12 cupcakes*

Coconut Lime Whipped Cream: Beat 1 cup whipping cream in large bowl with electric mixer at medium-high speed until soft peaks form. Add 2½ tablespoons well-shaken coconut milk, 1 tablespoon sugar and grated peel and juice of 1 lime; beat until stiff peaks form.

Spicy Coconut Lime Cupcakes

Cosmopolitan Cupcakes

    1 cup cranberry juice
    ¾ cup vodka
    ¼ cup orange juice
    Grated peel and juice of 2 limes
    1 package (about 18 ounces) white cake mix
    ⅓ cup vegetable oil
    2 eggs
    1 egg white
    Pink or red food coloring
    ½ cup (1 stick) butter, softened
    2 cups powdered sugar
    Coarse sugar (optional)

1. Preheat oven to 350°F. Line 22 standard (2½-inch) muffin cups with paper baking cups.

2. Combine cranberry juice, vodka, orange juice, lime peel and lime juice in large glass measuring cup; mix well.

3. Beat cake mix, 1 cup cranberry juice mixture, oil, eggs and egg white in large bowl with electric mixer at low speed until smooth. Add food coloring, a few drops at a time, until desired shade of pink is reached. Spoon batter evenly into prepared muffin cups.

4. Bake 20 minutes or until toothpick inserted into centers comes out clean. Brush warm cupcakes with ½ cup cranberry juice mixture. Remove to wire racks to cool completely.

5. Beat butter, remaining ½ cup cranberry juice mixture and powdered sugar in large bowl with electric mixer at medium speed until fluffy. Add food coloring, a few drops at a time, until desired shade of pink is reached.

6. Pipe or spread frosting on cupcakes; sprinkle with coarse sugar, if desired.

Makes 22 cupcakes

Cosmopolitan Cupcakes

Butter Pecan Cupcakes

2 cups chopped pecans
3 cups all-purpose flour
2 teaspoons baking powder
½ teaspoon salt
2 cups granulated sugar
1 cup (2 sticks) butter, softened
4 eggs
¾ cup milk
¼ cup vegetable oil
1½ teaspoons vanilla
Browned Butter Frosting (recipe follows)
Whole pecans (optional)

1. Preheat oven to 350°F. Line 30 standard (2½-inch) muffin cups with paper baking cups.

2. Spread chopped pecans in shallow baking pan. Bake 5 minutes or until lightly toasted, stirring occasionally. Transfer to plate; cool completely.

3. Whisk flour, baking powder and salt in medium bowl. Beat granulated sugar and butter in large bowl with electric mixer at medium speed until creamy. Add eggs, one at a time, beating well after each addition.

4. Combine milk, oil and vanilla in small bowl. Alternately add flour mixture and milk mixture to butter mixture, beating well after each addition. Stir in chopped pecans. Spoon batter evenly into prepared muffin cups.

5. Bake 20 minutes or until toothpick inserted into centers comes out clean. Cool cupcakes in pans 10 minutes; remove to wire racks to cool completely.

6. Prepare Browned Butter Frosting. Frost cupcakes; garnish with whole pecans.

Makes 30 cupcakes

Browned Butter Frosting: Melt 1 cup (2 sticks) butter in small saucepan over medium heat. Cook and stir until light brown. Remove from heat; let stand 10 minutes. Beat browned butter, 5½ cups powdered sugar, ¼ cup milk, 1½ teaspoons vanilla and ⅛ teaspoon salt in large bowl with electric mixer at medium speed until smooth. Add additional milk, 1 tablespoon at a time, if frosting is too stiff.

Butter Pecan Cupcakes

Limoncello Cupcakes

Cupcakes

- 1 package (about 18 ounces) lemon cake mix without pudding in the mix
- 1 package (4-serving size) lemon instant pudding and pie filling mix
- 4 eggs
- ½ cup vegetable oil
- ½ cup vodka
- ½ cup water

Glaze

- 4 cups powdered sugar
- ⅓ cup lemon juice
- 3 to 4 tablespoons vodka
- Candied lemon peel (optional)
- Coarse sugar (optional)

1. Preheat oven to 350°F. Line 22 standard (2½-inch) muffin cups with paper baking cups.

2. For cupcakes, beat cake mix, pudding mix, eggs, oil, ½ cup vodka and water in large bowl with electric mixer at low speed until smooth. Spoon batter evenly into prepared muffin cups.

3. Bake 18 minutes or until toothpick inserted into centers comes out clean. Cool cupcakes in pans 10 minutes; remove to wire racks to cool completely.

4. For glaze, whisk powdered sugar, lemon juice and 3 tablespoons vodka in medium bowl until smooth. Add remaining 1 tablespoon vodka if glaze is too stiff.

5. Dip tops of cupcakes in glaze; return to wire racks. Garnish with candied lemon peel; sprinkle with coarse sugar, if desired. Let stand until set.   *Makes 22 cupcakes*

Limoncello Cupcakes

Sweet & Salty Cupcakes

1¼ cups all-purpose flour
1 cup sugar
⅓ cup unsweetened Dutch process cocoa powder
1 teaspoon baking soda
½ teaspoon baking powder
½ teaspoon salt
½ cup buttermilk
½ cup coffee
¼ cup vegetable oil
1 egg
½ teaspoon vanilla
1 cup semisweet chocolate chips
½ cup whipping cream
¾ cup honey roasted peanuts, coarsely chopped
¾ cup coarsely chopped pretzels
¼ to ½ cup caramel topping

1. Preheat oven to 350°F. Line 12 standard (2½-inch) muffin cups with paper baking cups.

2. Combine flour, sugar, cocoa, baking soda, baking powder and salt in large bowl; mix well. Whisk buttermilk, coffee, oil, egg and vanilla in medium bowl until blended. Add to flour mixture; stir until well blended. Spoon batter evenly into prepared muffin cups.

3. Bake about 16 minutes or until toothpick inserted into centers comes out clean. Cool cupcakes in pan 5 minutes; remove to wire rack to cool completely.

4. Place chocolate chips in medium heatproof bowl. Heat cream to a simmer in small saucepan over medium heat. Pour cream over chocolate chips; let stand 5 minutes. Stir until blended and smooth. Set ganache aside about 20 minutes to thicken.

5. Dip tops of cupcakes in ganache; return to wire rack. Sprinkle with peanuts and pretzels. Let stand until set. Drizzle with caramel topping just before serving.   *Makes 12 cupcakes*

Tip: These cupcakes are best served the day they are made. Or you can prepare the cupcakes a day in advance and add the ganache and toppings the next day. The pretzels and peanuts become soggy if they are sprinkled on the cupcakes too early.

Sweet & Salty Cupcakes

Carrot Ginger Cupcakes

   1 pound carrots
   3 cups all-purpose flour
   ⅓ cup pecan chips
   2 teaspoons baking powder
   1 teaspoon baking soda
   1 teaspoon salt
   ½ teaspoon ground cinnamon
   1½ cups granulated sugar
   1¼ cups (2½ sticks) plus 2 tablespoons butter, softened, divided
   1 tablespoon honey
   4 eggs
      Grated peel of 2 oranges
      Juice of 1 orange
   1 tablespoon plus 1 teaspoon vanilla, divided
   1½ teaspoons grated fresh ginger
      1 package (8 ounces) cream cheese, softened
   ½ teaspoon orange extract
   3½ cups powdered sugar
      1 cup chopped pecans

1. Preheat oven to 350°F. Line 24 standard (2½-inch) muffin cups with paper baking cups.

2. Grate carrots in food processor; drain well. Whisk flour, pecan chips, baking powder, baking soda, salt and cinnamon in medium bowl.

3. Beat granulated sugar, 1 cup plus 2 tablespoons butter and honey in large bowl with electric mixer at medium speed until light and fluffy. Add eggs, one at a time, beating well after each addition. Add carrots, orange peel and juice, 1 tablespoon vanilla and ginger; mix well. Add flour mixture; mix just until combined. Spoon batter evenly into prepared muffin cups.

4. Bake 20 minutes or until toothpick inserted into centers comes out clean. Cool cupcakes in pans 10 minutes; remove to wire racks to cool completely.

5. Beat cream cheese, remaining ¼ cup butter, orange extract and remaining 1 teaspoon vanilla in medium bowl at medium speed until light and fluffy. Gradually add powdered sugar, beating until well blended.

6. Frost cupcakes; sprinkle with chopped pecans. Refrigerate until ready to serve.

Makes 24 cupcakes

Chocolate Bliss

Chocolate Malt Cupcakes

1 package (about 18 ounces) milk chocolate cake mix with pudding in the mix

2 cups (1 pint) chocolate ice cream, softened

3 eggs

¾ cup water

½ cup chocolate malted milk powder*

1 container (16 ounces) milk chocolate frosting

32 malted milk balls

You can find malted milk powder in the supermarket with ice cream toppings or powdered beverages.

1. Preheat oven to 350°F. Line 32 standard (2½-inch) muffin cups with paper baking cups.

2. Beat cake mix, ice cream, eggs, water and malted milk powder in large bowl with electric mixer at low speed 30 seconds. Beat at medium speed 2 minutes or until well blended. Spoon batter into prepared muffin cups, filling half full.

3. Bake 20 to 23 minutes or until toothpick inserted into centers comes out clean. Cool cupcakes in pans 10 minutes; remove to wire racks to cool completely.

4. Frost cupcakes; top with malted milk balls.

Makes 32 cupcakes

Double Peanut Butter Milk Chocolate Cupcakes

1 package (11½ ounces) milk chocolate chips, divided
¼ cup (½ stick) butter
1½ cups all-purpose flour
½ cup sugar
1 teaspoon baking powder
½ teaspoon salt
¾ cup buttermilk
2 eggs
1 teaspoon vanilla
42 mini chocolate peanut butter cups (¾ inch in diameter, not individually wrapped)
¼ cup whipping cream
¼ cup peanut butter

1. Preheat oven to 350°F. Line 42 mini (1¾-inch) muffin cups with paper baking cups.

2. Combine 1 cup chocolate chips and butter in medium microwavable bowl. Microwave on HIGH 30 seconds; stir. Repeat as necessary until chips are melted and mixture is smooth. Let cool slightly. Combine flour, sugar, baking powder and salt in large bowl. Whisk buttermilk, eggs and vanilla in small bowl until blended. Add buttermilk mixture and melted chocolate mixture to flour mixture; stir until well blended.

3. Fill prepared muffin cups half full with batter. Place one peanut butter cup in each muffin cup; top with remaining batter. (Cups will be almost full.)

4. Bake about 12 minutes or until toothpick inserted near centers comes out clean. Cool cupcakes in pans 5 minutes; remove to wire racks to cool completely.

5. Place remaining chocolate chips in medium heatproof bowl. Heat cream to a simmer in small saucepan over medium heat. Pour cream over chocolate chips; let stand 5 minutes. Stir until blended and smooth. Set ganache aside about 20 minutes to thicken.

6. Place peanut butter in small microwavable bowl. Microwave on MEDIUM (50%) about 15 seconds or just until softened. Dip tops of cupcakes in ganache; return to wire racks. Use toothpick to add streaks of softened peanut butter to ganache topping. Let stand until set.

Makes 42 mini cupcakes

·Chocolate Bliss·

Double Peanut Butter Milk Chocolate Cupcakes

Cream-Filled Cupcakes

1 package (about 18 ounces) dark chocolate cake mix, plus ingredients to prepare mix
½ cup (1 stick) butter, softened
¼ cup shortening
3 cups powdered sugar
1⅓ cups whipping cream, divided
1 teaspoon salt
2 cups semisweet chocolate chips

1. Preheat oven to 350°F. Line 22 standard (2½-inch) muffin cups with paper baking cups. Prepare cake mix according to package directions. Spoon batter into prepared muffin cups, filling two-thirds full.

2. Bake 20 minutes or until toothpick inserted into centers comes out clean. Cool cupcakes in pans 10 minutes; remove to wire racks to cool completely.

3. Beat butter and shortening in large bowl with electric mixer at medium speed until well blended. Add powdered sugar, ⅓ cup cream and salt; beat at low speed 1 minute. Beat at medium-high speed 2 minutes or until fluffy. Place filling in piping bag fitted with large round tip. Press tip into top of each cupcake and squeeze bag to fill. Reserve remaining filling.

4. Place chocolate chips in medium heatproof bowl. Heat remaining 1 cup cream to a simmer in small saucepan over medium heat. Pour cream over chocolate chips; let stand 5 minutes. Stir until blended and smooth. Set ganache aside about 20 minutes to thicken.

5. Dip tops of cupcakes in ganache; return to wire racks. Let stand until set. Pipe swirl design on top of ganache with reserved filling using small round tip.   *Makes 22 cupcakes*

Cream-Filled Cupcakes

Bittersweet Chocolate Raspberry Cupcakes

1½ cups all-purpose flour

1 teaspoon baking powder

1 teaspoon baking soda

½ teaspoon salt

¾ cup hot coffee

¾ cup unsweetened cocoa powder

8 ounces bittersweet chocolate, chopped, divided

1¼ cups sugar

2 eggs

⅓ cup vegetable oil

1 teaspoon vanilla

¾ cup buttermilk

2 pints fresh raspberries, divided

½ cup whipping cream

1. Preheat oven to 350°F. Line 20 standard (2½-inch) muffin cups with paper baking cups.

2. Combine flour, baking powder, baking soda and salt in small bowl. Combine coffee, cocoa and 2 ounces chopped chocolate in large bowl; whisk until chocolate is melted and mixture is smooth. Stir in sugar, eggs, oil and vanilla until well blended. Alternately add flour mixture and buttermilk; mix well. Spoon batter evenly into prepared muffin cups; place three raspberries in each cup.

3. Bake 22 minutes or until toothpick inserted into centers comes out clean. Cool cupcakes in pans 5 minutes; remove to wire racks to cool completely.

4. Place remaining 6 ounces chopped chocolate in medium heatproof bowl. Heat cream to a simmer in small saucepan over medium heat. Pour cream over chocolate; let stand 5 minutes. Stir until blended and smooth. Set ganache aside about 20 minutes to thicken.

5. Dip tops of cupcakes in ganache; return to wire racks. Top cupcakes with remaining raspberries. Let stand until set.

Makes 20 cupcakes

Bittersweet Chocolate Raspberry Cupcakes

Truffle Brownie Bites

¾ cup plus ⅔ cup semisweet chocolate chips, divided
½ cup (1 stick) butter, cut into chunks
1⅓ cups sugar
3 eggs
1 teaspoon vanilla
¾ cup plus 2 tablespoons all-purpose flour
½ teaspoon salt
¼ plus 2 tablespoons whipping cream
Colored sprinkles

1. Preheat oven to 350°F. Line 36 mini (1¾-inch) muffin cups with paper baking cups.

2. Combine ⅔ cup chocolate chips and butter in large microwavable bowl. Microwave on HIGH 30 seconds; stir. Repeat as necessary until chips are melted and mixture is smooth. Let cool slightly.

3. Add sugar to melted chocolate mixture; beat until well blended. Add eggs, one at a time, beating well after each addition. Stir in vanilla. Add flour and salt; beat until well blended. Spoon batter into prepared muffin cups, filling three-fourths full.

4. Bake 15 minutes or until tops are firm to the touch. Cool cupcakes in pans 5 minutes; remove to wire racks to cool completely.

5. Place remaining ¾ cup chocolate chips in medium heatproof bowl. Heat cream to a simmer in small saucepan over medium heat. Pour cream over chocolate chips; let stand 5 minutes. Stir until blended and smooth. Set ganache aside about 20 minutes to thicken.

6. Dip tops of cupcakes in ganache; return to wire racks. Decorate with sprinkles. Let stand until set.

Makes 36 mini cupcakes

Truffle Brownie Bites

Dark Chocolate Banana Cupcakes

1½ cups all-purpose flour
1½ cups granulated sugar
½ cup unsweetened Dutch process cocoa powder
2 tablespoons packed brown sugar
2 teaspoons baking powder
½ teaspoon salt
½ cup vegetable oil
2 eggs
¼ cup buttermilk
1 teaspoon vanilla
2 mashed bananas (about 1 cup)
2 cups dark chocolate chips
1 cup whipping cream
Dried banana chips (optional)

1. Preheat oven to 350°F. Line 18 standard (2½-inch) muffin cups with paper baking cups.

2. Whisk flour, granulated sugar, cocoa, brown sugar, baking powder and salt in large bowl. Add oil, eggs, buttermilk and vanilla; beat with electric mixer at medium speed 2 minutes or until well blended. Beat in bananas until well blended. Spoon batter into prepared muffin cups, filling three-fourths full.

3. Bake 25 minutes or until toothpick inserted into centers comes out clean. Cool cupcakes in pans 10 minutes; remove to wire racks to cool completely.

4. Place chocolate chips in medium heatproof bowl. Heat cream to a simmer in small saucepan over medium heat. Pour cream over chocolate chips; let stand 5 minutes. Stir until blended and smooth. Set ganache aside about 20 minutes to thicken.

5. Dip tops of cupcakes in ganache; return to wire racks. Drizzle banana chips with remaining ganache; arrange on cupcakes, if desired. Let stand until set.   *Makes 18 cupcakes*

Dark Chocolate Banana Cupcakes

Gooey Coconut Chocolate Cupcakes

1 package (about 18 ounces) chocolate cake mix, plus ingredients to prepare mix
½ cup (1 stick) butter
1 cup packed brown sugar
⅓ cup whipping cream, half-and-half or milk
1½ cups sweetened flaked coconut
½ cup chopped pecans (optional)

1. Preheat oven to 350°F. Line 22 standard (2½-inch) muffin cups with paper baking cups. Prepare cake mix according to package directions. Spoon batter into prepared muffin cups, filling two-thirds full.

2. Bake 20 minutes or until toothpick inserted into centers comes out clean. Do not remove cupcakes from pans.

3. Preheat broiler. Melt butter in medium saucepan over low heat. Stir in brown sugar and cream until well blended and sugar is dissolved. Add coconut and pecans, if desired; mix well. Spread 2 to 3 tablespoons coconut mixture over each cupcake.

4. Place cupcakes under broiler 2 to 3 minutes or until tops begin to brown and edges bubble. Cool cupcakes in pans 5 minutes; remove to wire racks. Serve warm or at room temperature.

Makes 22 cupcakes

Gooey Coconut Chocolate Cupcakes

Tutti Frutti

Raspberry Layer Cupcakes

2 cups all-purpose flour
2½ teaspoons baking powder
½ teaspoon salt
1 cup milk
1 teaspoon vanilla

1½ cups granulated sugar
½ cup (1 stick) butter, softened
3 eggs
1½ cups seedless raspberry jam
Powdered sugar

1. Preheat oven to 350°F. Spray 18 standard (2½-inch) muffin cups with nonstick cooking spray.

2. Combine flour, baking powder and salt in medium bowl. Combine milk and vanilla in small bowl. Beat granulated sugar and butter in large bowl with electric mixer at medium speed about 3 minutes or until creamy. Add eggs, one at a time, beating well after each addition. Add flour mixture alternately with milk mixture, beating until well blended. Spoon batter into prepared muffin cups, filling three-fourths full.

3. Bake 18 to 20 minutes or until toothpick inserted into centers comes out clean. Cool cupcakes in pans 10 minutes; remove to wire racks to cool completely.

4. Cut cupcakes in thirds crosswise. Spread about 2 teaspoons jam over bottom layer. Top with second layer; spread with 2 teaspoons jam. Top with third layer of cupcake; sprinkle with powdered sugar.

Makes 18 cupcakes

Lemon Buttons

¾ cup all-purpose flour
½ teaspoon baking powder
¼ teaspoon baking soda
¼ teaspoon salt
½ cup granulated sugar
¼ cup (½ stick) butter, softened
1 egg
¾ teaspoon grated lemon peel
2½ tablespoons lemon juice, divided
¼ cup milk
¾ cup powdered sugar, sifted
  Yellow and pink food coloring
  Yellow and pink sugar pearls

1. Preheat oven to 350°F. Line 30 mini (1¾-inch) muffin cups with paper baking cups.

2. Combine flour, baking powder, baking soda and salt in small bowl. Beat granulated sugar and butter in medium bowl with electric mixer at medium speed until creamy. Add egg, lemon peel and 1½ tablespoons lemon juice; beat until well blended. Add flour mixture; beat at low speed while adding milk just until combined. Spoon batter into prepared muffin cups, filling half full.

3. Bake about 10 minutes or until toothpick inserted into centers comes out clean. Cool cupcakes in pans 5 minutes; remove to wire racks to cool completely.

4. For glaze, whisk powdered sugar and remaining 1 tablespoon lemon juice in small bowl until smooth. Divide glaze between two bowls; add food coloring, a few drops at a time, until desired shades are reached. Dip top of each cupcake in glaze to coat (coating should be thick); scrape off excess glaze on edge of bowl. Let cupcakes stand about 1 hour or until glaze is set.

5. Press 1¼-inch round cookie cutter into top of each cupcake to score circle in glaze. Arrange sugar pearls in center of each cupcake for buttonholes. (Or omit sugar pearls; use toothpick to poke four holes in center of each cupcake for buttonholes.) *Makes 30 mini cupcakes*

Tip: If your cupcakes have domes after baking, cool them upside down on a sheet of parchment paper to flatten the tops.

Lemon Buttons

Blueberry Buttermilk Cupcakes

¾ cup fresh blueberries, plus additional for garnish
1¾ cups all-purpose flour
2 teaspoons baking powder
½ teaspoon salt
¼ teaspoon baking soda
½ cup granulated sugar
¼ cup (½ stick) butter, softened
1 egg
Grated peel of 1 lemon
1 tablespoon plus 1 teaspoon lemon juice, divided
1 cup plus 2 tablespoons buttermilk, divided
1½ to 2 cups powdered sugar

1. Freeze ¾ cup blueberries 30 minutes to firm. Preheat oven to 350°F. Line 12 standard (2½-inch) muffin cups with paper baking cups.

2. Place frozen blueberries in food processor; process until finely chopped.

3. Combine flour, baking powder, salt and baking soda in small bowl. Beat granulated sugar and butter in large bowl with electric mixer at medium speed until creamy. Add egg, lemon peel and 1 tablespoon lemon juice; beat until blended. Beat in flour mixture, 1 cup buttermilk and chopped blueberries at low speed just until combined. Spoon batter evenly into prepared muffin cups.

4. Bake 20 minutes or until toothpick inserted into centers comes out clean. Cool cupcakes in pan 5 minutes; remove to wire rack to cool completely.

5. Whisk remaining 2 tablespoons buttermilk, 1 teaspoon lemon juice and 1½ cups powdered sugar in medium bowl until smooth. Add additional powdered sugar, if necessary, to reach desired icing consistency.

6. Dip tops of cupcakes in icing to coat; return to wire rack. Garnish cupcakes with additional blueberries; drizzle with remaining icing. Let stand until set. *Makes 12 cupcakes*

Blueberry Buttermilk Cupcakes

Peaches & Cream Cupcakes

    1 cup all-purpose flour
¼ cup cornmeal
    1 teaspoon baking powder
½ teaspoon baking soda
½ teaspoon salt
¾ cup granulated sugar
½ cup (1 stick) butter, softened
    2 eggs
1½ teaspoons vanilla, divided
⅓ cup buttermilk
    1 large ripe peach, peeled and finely chopped (about 1 cup)
½ cup peach jam
    1 cup whipping cream
    1 tablespoon powdered sugar
    1 medium ripe peach, chopped

1. Preheat oven to 350°F. Line 12 standard (2½-inch) muffin cups with paper baking cups.

2. Combine flour, cornmeal, baking powder, baking soda and salt in medium bowl. Beat granulated sugar and butter in large bowl with electric mixer at medium speed until creamy. Add eggs and 1 teaspoon vanilla; beat until well blended. Add flour mixture; beat at low speed while adding buttermilk. Beat just until combined. Stir in finely chopped peach. Spoon batter into prepared muffin cups, filling two-thirds full.

3. Bake 20 to 22 minutes or until toothpick inserted into centers comes out clean. Cool cupcakes in pan 5 minutes; remove to wire rack to cool completely.

4. Cut 1-inch hole in top of each cupcake, reserving cupcake pieces. Fill each hole with 2 teaspoons peach jam; replace cupcake piece.

5. Beat cream in large bowl with electric mixer at medium-high speed until soft peaks form. Add powdered sugar and remaining ½ teaspoon vanilla; beat until stiff peaks form. Top cupcakes with whipped cream; garnish with chopped peach.   *Makes 12 cupcakes*

Peaches & Cream Cupcakes

Cream Cheese Cupcakes

   3 packages (8 ounces each) cream cheese, softened
   5 eggs
1¼ cups sugar, divided
2½ teaspoons vanilla, divided
   1 container (16 ounces) sour cream
   1 cup chopped fresh pitted cherries, fresh blueberries and canned crushed pineapple, drained

1. Preheat oven to 325°F. Line 24 standard (2½-inch) muffin cups with paper baking cups.

2. Beat cream cheese, eggs, 1 cup sugar and 1½ teaspoons vanilla in large bowl with electric mixer at medium speed 2 minutes or until well blended. Spoon batter into prepared muffin cups, filling three-fourths full.

3. Bake 20 minutes or until light golden brown. Cool cupcakes in pans 5 minutes. (Centers of cupcakes will sink slightly.) Do not remove cupcakes from pans.

4. Meanwhile, combine sour cream, remaining ¼ cup sugar and 1 teaspoon vanilla in medium bowl; stir until blended. Fill depression in cupcakes with sour cream mixture. Bake 5 minutes. Cool cupcakes in pans 10 minutes; remove to wire racks to cool completely.

5. Top cupcakes with desired fruit topping.

Makes 24 cupcakes

Cream Cheese Cupcakes

Apple Cheddar Cupcakes

Cheddar Streusel Topping (recipe follows)
1 cup all-purpose flour
½ teaspoon baking powder
½ teaspoon baking soda
½ teaspoon salt
6 tablespoons butter, softened
½ cup granulated sugar
¼ cup packed brown sugar
1 egg
1 teaspoon vanilla
½ cup milk
1 cup finely chopped Granny Smith apple
½ cup (2 ounces) finely shredded sharp Cheddar cheese

1. Prepare Cheddar Streusel Topping. Preheat oven to 350°F. Line 36 mini (1¾-inch) muffin cups with paper baking cups.

2. Combine flour, baking powder, baking soda and salt in small bowl. Beat butter, granulated sugar and brown sugar in large bowl with electric mixer at medium speed until creamy. Add egg and vanilla; beat until well blended. Add flour mixture and milk; stir just until combined. Stir in apple and cheese.

3. Spoon batter into prepared muffin cups, filling about half full. Sprinkle evenly with topping.

4. Bake 15 minutes or until toothpick inserted into centers comes out clean. Cool cupcakes in pans 5 minutes; remove to wire racks. Serve warm or at room temperature.

Makes 36 mini cupcakes

Cheddar Streusel Topping: Combine ⅓ cup all-purpose flour, 2 tablespoons melted butter, 2 tablespoons finely shredded sharp Cheddar cheese and 1 tablespoon granulated sugar in medium bowl; stir with fork until small crumbles form.

Apple Cheddar Cupcakes

Pineapple Upside-Down Cupcakes

1 can (20 ounces) pineapple chunks in syrup
1 cup packed brown sugar
1 package (about 18 ounces) yellow cake mix, plus ingredients to prepare mix
12 maraschino cherries, halved

1. Preheat oven to 350°F. Spray 24 standard (2½-inch) muffin cups with nonstick cooking spray. Drain pineapple, reserving ¼ cup syrup.

2. Place 2 teaspoons brown sugar in each prepared muffin cup. Cut 2 pineapple chunks horizontally to create 4 wedge-shaped pieces. Arrange pineapple pieces over brown sugar to resemble flower petals.

3. Prepare cake mix according to package directions, substituting ¼ cup pineapple syrup for ¼ cup water called for in package directions. Spoon batter over pineapple in muffin cups, filling three-fourths full.

4. Bake 20 minutes or until toothpick inserted into centers comes out clean. Cool cupcakes in pans 10 minutes; invert pans onto serving plates. Place cherry half in center of each cupcake.

Makes 24 cupcakes

Pineapple Upside-Down Cupcakes

Banana Cream Pie Cupcakes

1 package (about 18 ounces) yellow cake mix, plus ingredients to prepare mix
1 package (4-serving size) banana instant pudding and pie filling mix
2 cups milk
2 bananas
2 tablespoons sugar, divided
2 cups whipping cream

1. Preheat oven to 350°F. Line 24 standard (2½-inch) muffin cups with paper baking cups. Prepare cake mix according to package directions. Spoon batter evenly into prepared muffin cups.

2. Bake 20 minutes or until toothpick inserted into centers comes out clean. Cool cupcakes in pans 10 minutes; remove to wire racks to cool completely.

3. Prepare pudding using milk according to package directions. Cover and refrigerate until set.

4. Preheat broiler. Line baking sheet with parchment paper. Cut each banana into 12 slices. Place 1 tablespoon sugar in shallow bowl. Dip one side of each banana slice into sugar; place sugar side up on prepared baking sheet. Broil 2 minutes or until golden brown. Cool completely.

5. Beat cream and remaining 1 tablespoon sugar in large bowl with electric mixer at medium-high speed until stiff peaks form.

6. Cut 1-inch hole in top of each cupcake; discard cupcake pieces. Fill holes with pudding (reserve remaining pudding for another use). Pipe or spread whipped cream over filling. Top cupcakes with banana slices.

Makes 24 cupcakes

•Index•

METRIC CONVERSION CHART

VOLUME MEASUREMENTS (dry)

$\frac{1}{8}$ teaspoon = 0.5 mL
$\frac{1}{4}$ teaspoon = 1 mL
$\frac{1}{2}$ teaspoon = 2 mL
$\frac{3}{4}$ teaspoon = 4 mL
1 teaspoon = 5 mL
1 tablespoon = 15 mL
2 tablespoons = 30 mL
$\frac{1}{4}$ cup = 60 mL
$\frac{1}{3}$ cup = 75 mL
$\frac{1}{2}$ cup = 125 mL
$\frac{2}{3}$ cup = 150 mL
$\frac{3}{4}$ cup = 175 mL
1 cup = 250 mL
2 cups = 1 pint = 500 mL
3 cups = 750 mL
4 cups = 1 quart = 1 L

VOLUME MEASUREMENTS (fluid)

1 fluid ounce (2 tablespoons) = 30 mL
4 fluid ounces ($\frac{1}{2}$ cup) = 125 mL
8 fluid ounces (1 cup) = 250 mL
12 fluid ounces ($1\frac{1}{2}$ cups) = 375 mL
16 fluid ounces (2 cups) = 500 mL

WEIGHTS (mass)

$\frac{1}{2}$ ounce = 15 g
1 ounce = 30 g
3 ounces = 90 g
4 ounces = 120 g
8 ounces = 225 g
10 ounces = 285 g
12 ounces = 360 g
16 ounces = 1 pound = 450 g

DIMENSIONS

$\frac{1}{16}$ inch = 2 mm
$\frac{1}{8}$ inch = 3 mm
$\frac{1}{4}$ inch = 6 mm
$\frac{1}{2}$ inch = 1.5 cm
$\frac{3}{4}$ inch = 2 cm
1 inch = 2.5 cm

OVEN TEMPERATURES

250°F = 120°C
275°F = 140°C
300°F = 150°C
325°F = 160°C
350°F = 180°C
375°F = 190°C
400°F = 200°C
425°F = 220°C
450°F = 230°C

BAKING PAN SIZES

Utensil	Size in Inches/Quarts	Metric Volume	Size in Centimeters
Baking or Cake Pan (square or rectangular)	8×8×2	2 L	20×20×5
	9×9×2	2.5 L	23×23×5
	12×8×2	3 L	30×20×5
	13×9×2	3.5 L	33×23×5
Loaf Pan	8×4×3	1.5 L	20×10×7
	9×5×3	2 L	23×13×7
Round Layer Cake Pan	8×1½	1.2 L	20×4
	9×1½	1.5 L	23×4
Pie Plate	8×1¼	750 mL	20×3
	9×1¼	1 L	23×3
Baking Dish or Casserole	1 quart	1 L	—
	1½ quart	1.5 L	—
	2 quart	2 L	—